Landmarks
Around the World

Lorin Driggs

Consultants

Andrea Johnson, Ph.D.
Assistant Professor of History
California State University, Dominguez Hills

Eileen Marthiensen, M.Ed.
Teacher, Alberta, Canada

Brian Allman
Principal
Upshur County Schools, West Virginia

Olivia Tolich
Subject Matter Expert, K–6
Pearson Australia

Publishing Credits

Rachelle Cracchiolo, M.S.Ed., *Publisher*
Emily R. Smith, M.A.Ed., *SVP of Content Development*
Véronique Bos, *Vice President of Creative*
Dani Neiley, *Editor*
Fabiola Sepulveda, *Series Graphic Designer*

Image Credits: p.4 Shutterstock/TJ Brown; p.5 Shutterstock/Grobler du Preez; p.7 Alamy Stock Photo/World History Archive; p.15 © Easter Island Statue Project/Jo Anne Van Tilburg; p.17 (top) © Look and Learn/Bridgeman Images; p.17 (bottom) Shutterstock/Wizdata; p.21 (bottom) Shutterstock/Rudy Mareel; p.24 Getty Images/Jurgen Schadeberg; p.32 Library of Congress [LC-DIG-krb-00001]; all other images from iStock and/or Shutterstock

Library of Congress Cataloging-in-Publication Data

Names: Driggs, Lorin, author.
Title: Landmarks around the world / Lorin Driggs.
Description: Huntington Beach, CA : Teacher Created Materials, [2023] |
  Includes index. | Audience: Ages 8-18 | Summary: "Take a trip around the
  world. See spectacular landmarks created by Earth's natural forces.
  Marvel at massive pyramids built thousands of years ago. Visit an island
  where huge carved heads look out over the land. Explore beautiful modern
  landmarks. Learn how technology has changed what people can imagine and
  what they can build"-- Provided by publisher.
Identifiers: LCCN 2022038418 (print) | LCCN 2022038419 (ebook) | ISBN
  9781087695235 (paperback) | ISBN 9781087695396 (ebook)
Subjects: LCSH: Historic sites--Juvenile literature. | Natural
  monuments--Juvenile literature. | Structural engineering--Juvenile
  literature. | Curiosities and wonders--Juvenile literature.
Classification: LCC CC135 .D75 2023 (print) | LCC CC135 (ebook) | DDC
  910.9--dc23/eng/20220913
LC record available at https://lccn.loc.gov/2022038418
LC ebook record available at https://lccn.loc.gov/2022038419

**Shown on the cover is
Angkor Wat, Cambodia.**

TCM Teacher
Created
Materials

5482 Argosy Avenue
Huntington Beach, CA 92649
www.tcmpub.com
ISBN 978-1-0876-9523-5
© 2023 Teacher Created Materials, Inc.

Table of Contents

northern lights in Yellowknife, Canada

So Much to See

The world is full of landmarks. These are objects or features that are easily seen and recognized. Landmarks help tell people where they are. They help people remember special places.

Some landmarks are natural. They are formed by the earth's natural processes. Flowing rivers, falling rain, and melting snow change the shape of the land. Wind changes it, too. These changes have been happening for millions of years.

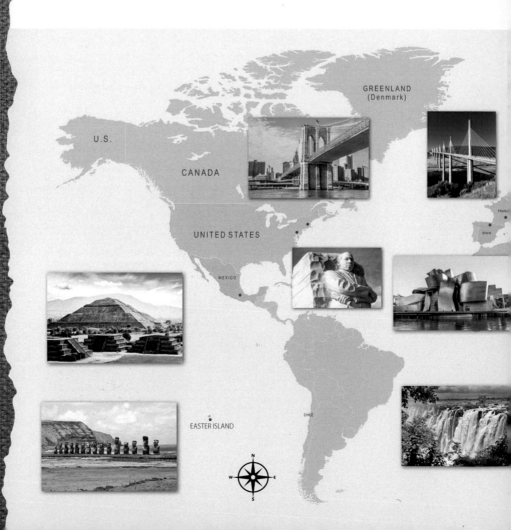

Other landmarks were made by people thousands of years ago. Human beings have always used their imaginations and their intelligence to design and build special places. Even before they had power tools and machines to help them, they created spectacular buildings and **monuments**. Many of those ancient structures have survived and are still standing.

Other landmarks were made by people in modern times. Today, we have modern technology to help create buildings and monuments. Machines do the hard work that human hands once did. People use technology to figure out how to turn things they imagine into reality.

RUSSIA

CHINA

EGYPT

ZAMBIA

SOUTH
AFRICA

AUSTRALIA

Natural Wonders

Landmarks are like stories. They reveal information about places. This is especially true when they are created by nature itself.

Victoria Falls

Imagine you are in southern Africa. You are following the Zambezi River along the border between Zambia and Zimbabwe. Your destination is one of the greatest natural landmarks in the world. It is still far away, but you can already hear its mighty roar. As you get closer, you see what looks like smoke rising ahead. Closer still, you feel a great rumbling under your feet. Finally, you are there! A waterfall more than 1 mile (1.6 kilometers) across stretches before you. The sheet of falling water roars. Mist rises like smoke. The force of water crashing into the river below rumbles through the earth.

1857 drawing of Victoria Falls

This place is known by several names. Its Indigenous name translates to "The Smoke That Thunders." Its name in English is Victoria Falls.

Victoria Falls is a popular tourist attraction for the people of Africa. It also draws visitors from all over the world. **Political** conflicts and wars in the past sometimes interrupted tourism. Today, the main threat is climate change. Scientists have predicted that more and more **droughts** could eventually slow or even stop the flow of water over the falls.

Landmarks Come and Go

In 225 BCE, a writer created a list of "seven wonders." They came to be known as the Seven Wonders of the Ancient World. Only one—the Great Pyramid of Giza—still exists. The others were destroyed by natural forces or by people during wars.

The Great Barrier Reef

The Great Barrier Reef is located off the coast of Australia. It is the world's largest coral reef **ecosystem**. It stretches more than 1,250 miles (2,000 kilometers). Like all coral reefs, it is a living thing. Coral reefs are formed mainly by tiny creatures called *polyps*. Living coral polyps attach themselves to the skeletons of dead polyps on the reef. When they die, their bodies harden into skeletons. The reef grows as more and more polyps attach themselves.

The Great Barrier Reef has the most **diverse** reef ecosystem in the world. There are 450 species of hard coral at the reef. Scientists have found that more than 1,500 species of fish live there. Fish rely on the reef for shelter. They also find food and raise their young on the reef.

aerial view of the Great Barrier Reef

latticed butterflyfish

Healthy coral reefs are beautiful. That is one reason the Great Barrier Reef is popular with tourists. More than 60,000 people have jobs associated with the reef. Tourists need tour guides to visit the reef. They have to take boats to get there. Fishing and diving equipment are also needed. Plus, tourists need places to stay and places to eat. This has created jobs that are good for Australia's **economy**. It is a delicate balance, though. If tourists accidentally damage the reef, the fragile environment becomes stressed. This causes harm to the coral.

What's Happening to Reefs?

Coral reefs around the world are in trouble. Ocean pollution is one problem. Climate change is another. These and other threats put stress on coral reefs. Stress can cause coral polyps to die. Scientists are working on ways to help protect healthy reefs and rebuild damaged ones.

dead coral reef

Northern Lights: A Natural Wonder

The northern lights are not a landmark, but they are still a natural wonder. They are also called the aurora borealis, which means "dawn of the north." They can be seen in many places. And you cannot always count on seeing them even if you go to those places. They are as beautiful as they are mysterious.

The northern lights are shimmering, colorful bands of light waving and bending across the sky. Some people describe them as curtains of dancing colored light.

Explaining the Northern Lights

There are many Inuit legends about the northern lights. One legend says the northern lights are spirits playing a ball game in the sky. Their tradition says the lights are caused by the spirits of dead people playing ball with the skull of a walrus.

Scientists have figured out that the colorful display is caused by light particles from the sun hitting Earth's atmosphere. Earth is surrounded by a **magnetic field**. When light particles from the sun hit that magnetic field, a light show happens. The magnetic field around the North Pole is very strong. That's why the best places to see the northern lights are in the far north. You would have a good chance of seeing them in Alaska, Norway, Sweden, Finland, Greenland, and northern Canada. The best time to see the lights is on a dark, clear night.

The South Pole also has a strong magnetic field. So, the same kind of lights can show up there. The southern lights are called *aurora australis*, or "dawn of the south."

southern lights

Gifts from People of the Past

Many magnificent sights around the world were created by people long ago. These landmarks were built without modern machines or materials. Still, they have lasted for thousands of years.

Pyramids of Giza

Three huge pyramids stand in the desert near the city of Giza, Egypt. Egyptians built the Pyramids of Giza more than 4,000 years ago. The pyramids were tombs, which are burial places designed to protect the bodies of dead pharaohs.

The largest pyramid was constructed of more than two million huge stones. It was originally 482 feet (147 meters) high. The stones are stacked precisely to form smooth, even sides that meet in a point at the top.

Menkaure

Khafre

Khufu (Great Pyramid of Giza)

Queen's Pyramids

illustration of Egyptians building a pyramid

The people of ancient Egypt built the pyramids without the help of bulldozers, trucks, or cranes. They could not use computers to help with design. They could not order supplies on the internet. Experts have tried to figure out how the Egyptians could have built these monumental structures. Clearly, it took a lot of people working very hard. Workers used hand tools to cut the stones out of rock. The stones were then probably loaded onto big sleds known as **sledges**. Then, workers pulled the heavy load to the building site. How were the stones lifted into place? This answer is still unclear.

Pyramid Builders around the World

Egyptians were not the only people to build pyramids. People in other parts of Africa built pyramids. The Maya and Aztec people of Central America built them, too. So did the Inka of South America. Indigenous peoples built the Pyramid of the Sun and the Pyramid of the Moon in Mexico. Many of these pyramids are still standing.

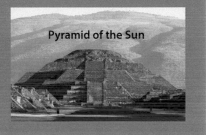
Pyramid of the Sun

The *Moai* of Rapa Nui, Chile

Imagine you are on a boat approaching a small island in the southern Pacific Ocean. As you get closer, large shapes appear along the coastline. Closer still, you see that they are all the shape of humans with huge heads. These are the *moai* (MOH-eye) on the island of Rapa Nui. *Moai* means "statue." This island is also known as Easter Island. Dutch explorers called it that because they reached the island on Easter Sunday.

These statues instantly raise questions. Who made them? How did they make them? How did they move them? How did they get them to stand upright? Some of these questions have been answered by **archaeologists** and other experts. Some questions are still a mystery.

The statues were created centuries ago. Experts believe they were created by the Rapa Nui people to honor powerful leaders from the past. They were carved in a **quarry**. Some were moved to their current locations. Others are still in the quarry. Almost 900 *moai* have been located by archaeologists. More may still be discovered.

The **inhabitants** of Rapa Nui who created the *moai* arrived more than 1,000 years ago. Today, **descendants** of the original people still live on Rapa Nui. The island's economy is based largely on tourism to see the *moai*.

On average, the *moai* are 13 feet (4 meters) tall.

Rapa Nui National Park

More to the Story

The *moai* are often described as heads, but they probably have bodies. Scientists believe the *moai* bodies were buried over time by soil that washed down from the hills on the island. The tallest *moai* above ground is 33 feet (10 meters) high.

The Great Wall of China

The Great Wall of China is "great" for several reasons. It was 13,171 miles (21,196 kilometers) long when it was first built. In comparison, the distance between the North Pole and the South Pole is only about 12,400 miles (19,956 kilometers)! The Great Wall is really a series of walls. Construction began almost 3,000 years ago. At that time, different parts of China had different rulers. The rulers built walls to keep enemies out. Over time, more sections were added. Today, large sections of the wall have **eroded**. These parts are in ruins. But there are some portions that are still in good condition.

A "Sticky" Solution

A mixture of lime powder and sticky rice is used to hold bricks together in the Great Wall. The mixture has been strong enough to survive earthquakes. It has helped many other Chinese structures survive for centuries, too.

No one knows for sure how many people worked on the Great Wall. But the work was very hard. It was also very dangerous.

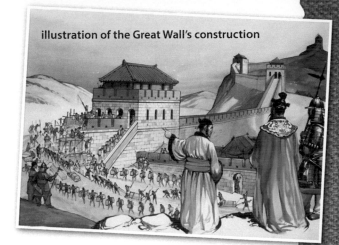
illustration of the Great Wall's construction

Signal towers were built along the wall. Soldiers used them to look for **invaders**. When they spotted enemies, the soldiers sent signals to guards on other towers. They communicated using smoke during the day and fire at night.

Today, the Great Wall is a symbol of China's long history. It represents Chinese **culture**. It is also a symbol of strength. Millions of tourists visit every year. When leaders from other countries visit China, they sometimes visit the Great Wall, too.

Angkor Wat, Cambodia

If you flew over Angkor Wat, you would see a wide **moat** creating a four-sided island. You would see five temples with elaborately carved spires. You would see thousands of other buildings spread out over 400 acres (160 hectares). Angkor Wat is the largest religious monument on Earth. The design and style are unique to the Khmer people of Cambodia.

Angkor Wat means "city of temples." It was built almost 900 years ago as a Hindu religious center. Later, it became a center for Buddhism. Both religions are still practiced in Cambodia. Descendants of the designers and builders still live nearby.

The five central towers represent the five peaks of Mount Meru. That is a **sacred** place for Hindus and Buddhists. In religion, it is said to be the center of the universe and the home of the gods.

Angkor Wat is full of magnificent works of art. There are carvings on walls. There are sculptures and paintings. They help tell the story of the lives and beliefs of the Khmer people long ago.

Bayon Temple has stone faces carved into pillars.

In a typical year, more than 2 million people visit Angkor Wat and the surrounding area. It is a popular religious and tourist destination. An image of Angkor Wat is even shown on the Cambodian flag.

A Very Special Tree

A type of fig tree is sacred in Hinduism and Buddhism. It is sometimes called the "strangler fig." Sometimes, its roots grow over other trees and kill them. They have also grown over buildings, including some temples in the Angkor region.

The Guggenheim is home to hundreds of works of modern art.

Modern Landmarks

For designers and builders today, what used to be impossible is now possible. Technology and science are part of every phase of their work. New materials are stronger. There are few limits to creating what can be imagined.

The Guggenheim Museum, Spain

In Bilbao, Spain, a building gleams in the sunlight next to a river. This is the Guggenheim Museum Bilbao. Its sides twist and curve. Sheets of titanium cover the building. This type of metal is hard but light. It does not rust. It appears to change color depending on weather and light conditions. **Architects** from around the world have praised it. One called it "the greatest building of our time."

The interior of the museum is as striking as the exterior. Curved walkways, elevators, and staircases connect three levels. The galleries have irregular shapes. The museum's website explains that this provides variety so visitors do not feel overwhelmed.

More than one million people now visit Bilbao each year.
Tourists enjoy the Guggenheim Museum. There are many
works of art inside. They are shown in 20 different galleries.
Some of these are permanent. This means they stay at the
museum. Other exhibits are temporary. People can go see the
artwork for a limited time.
This allows the museum to
showcase different artists.
It also gives people the
chance to come back and
see new artwork.

Super Spider

Many works of art are displayed outside of the Guggenheim
Museum in Bilbao. One of them is a giant spider sculpture
created by artist Louise Bourgeois. It is made of bronze,
stainless steel, and marble. It is over 30 feet (9.1 meters) high.

The Millau Viaduct, France

Landmarks can take many forms. They can be impressive buildings. They can be spectacular natural places. They can also be bridges that look like works of art.

The Millau **Viaduct** is famous for its beauty. It is also remarkable for the design that made it possible. The tallest part of the bridge is more than 1,125 feet (342.9 meters) above the ground, earning it the record as the tallest bridge in the world.

This beautiful bridge was built to solve a very common problem: traffic. Many people in France drive to the southern part of the country or to Spain for their summer vacations. Near the town of Millau, the winding roads went down into a valley. They then climbed back up again before continuing south. This caused a lot of traffic jams. It was clear that a bridge across the valley would solve the problem. The challenge was to design a bridge high enough and strong enough. A British architect and a French **structural engineer** came up with the plan. Construction began in 2001. The bridge opened in 2004.

Besides being a route for cars, the bridge is a popular landmark for tourists. It has a visitor center with exhibits about the design and construction. The visitor center also provides great views for taking pictures of the bridge.

The Millau Viaduct is made of steel and concrete.

construction of the Brooklyn Bridge

A Tale of Two Bridges

Building the Millau Viaduct took three years. More than 130 years earlier, building the Brooklyn Bridge in New York City took 14 years. The Brooklyn Bridge rises to approximately 272 feet (82.9 meters) at its highest point.

Nelson Mandela Sculpture, South Africa

In 1962, the police stopped a car traveling on a road in South Africa. The police arrested the man for his political activism. That man was Nelson Mandela. He spent the next 27 years in prison.

Mandela became known around the world while he was in prison. He was the leader of a movement. He fought to win equal rights for more than half of the people in South Africa. South Africa had a system known as **apartheid**. It made it legal to discriminate against the mostly Black majority and other non-white people. It gave all power in the government to the white minority. Mandela and others fought against this.

Mandela was finally freed in 1990. Four years later, he was elected president of South Africa. That election was the first time ever that Black South Africans had the right to vote.

On that road where the police arrested Mandela, a tribute now stands. It was created by artist Marco Cianfanelli. The sculpture is called "Release." Seen from some angles, the sculpture looks like a series of tall and jagged steel bars. But seen from just the right angle, the face of Nelson Mandela appears. The bars represent the prison where Mandela spent all those years. They also show the man who did not let bars silence him.

Nelson Mandela revisits his prison cell.

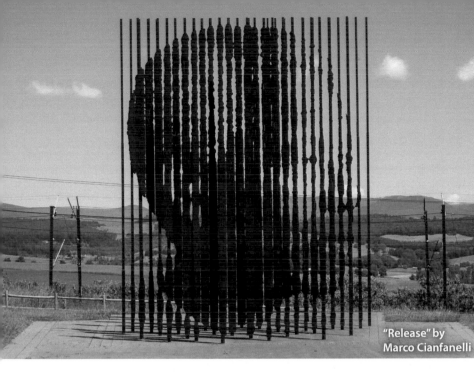

"Release" by
Marco Cianfanelli

A Stone of Hope

Martin Luther King Jr. was a leader of the civil rights movement
in the United States. A granite statue of him stands tall in
Washington, DC. Quotations from his life are engraved in the
monument. The statue includes part of his famous "I Have a
Dream" speech. The full quotation is, "With this faith, we will
be able to hew out of the mountain of despair a stone of hope."

The Legacy of Landmarks

You can see landmarks in many places all around the world. They take many forms.

Some landmarks are created by and from the earth alone. In these cases, nature forms something that amazes us.

Some landmarks were created by people long ago. Without machines or other technology, people used skill, determination, imagination, and intelligence to make things that have lasted over time. Those landmarks show how people from the past lived. They tell what those people knew and believed. They tell what was important to people of a different time. Some of these landmarks have survived the tests of time and weather.

Great Sphinx of Giza, Egypt

Eiffel Tower, France

Some landmarks have been created using modern technology. People can now use their intelligence and creativity to make things bigger, stronger, more useful, and more beautiful. When we see these landmarks, we might wonder if there are any limits to what people can create. If someone can imagine it, it can probably be made.

What landmarks would you like to see? Where in the world will you go to see them? If you could create a landmark, what would it be?

A Surprising Connection

The Statue of Liberty in New York City was a gift from the people of France. The Eiffel Tower in Paris, France, is a very famous landmark. Part of the statue was designed by the person who also designed the Eiffel Tower.

Map It!

Work with a small group to make a map for tourists traveling from your community to one of the landmarks featured in this book.

1. Choose a country that the tourists will travel to. Draw the outline of the country. Mark and label the specific destination in the country.

2. Write a brief description of the location. Give your map a title.

3. Create labels and small drawings, or graphics, to show at least three other landmarks in the country. For example, is there an important museum? Label it, and draw a picture of a building to mark it on your map.

4. Label any important bodies of water. Label the capital, too.

5. When your map is finished, pair up with another group. Present your map to them. Read the description you wrote, and explain why you chose the landmarks on your map.

Cairo and the Nile River

Egypt

Giza

Cairo

Nile River

Valley of the Kings

Luxor

Abu Simbel

Glossary

apartheid—a former policy of segregation and discrimination against non-white people in South Africa

archaeologists—scientists who learn about past human life by studying objects that ancient people left behind

architects—people who design buildings

culture—the beliefs, customs, arts, etc. of a particular society, group, place, or time

descendants—people who are related to a person or group of people who lived in the past

diverse—made up of people or things that are different from one another

droughts—long periods of time with little or no rain

economy—the system of making, selling, and buying goods and services in a particular place

ecosystem—a group of living and nonliving things that make up an environment and affect each other

eroded—worn away over time by the action of water, wind, or glacial ice

inhabitants—people who live in a particular place

invaders—people who enter a place to take control by force

magnetic field—an area that is influenced by magnetic force

moat—a deep, wide ditch filled with water that goes around a place to protect it from being attacked

monuments—buildings, statues, or places that honor a person or an event

political—relating to politics or government

quarry—a place where large amounts of stone are dug out of the ground

sacred—highly valued or important for religious reasons

sledges—large sleds for moving heavy objects

structural engineer—a person with scientific training for designing and building complicated buildings, bridges, and other structures

viaduct—a long, high bridge that carries a road or railroad over a valley, river, or something else